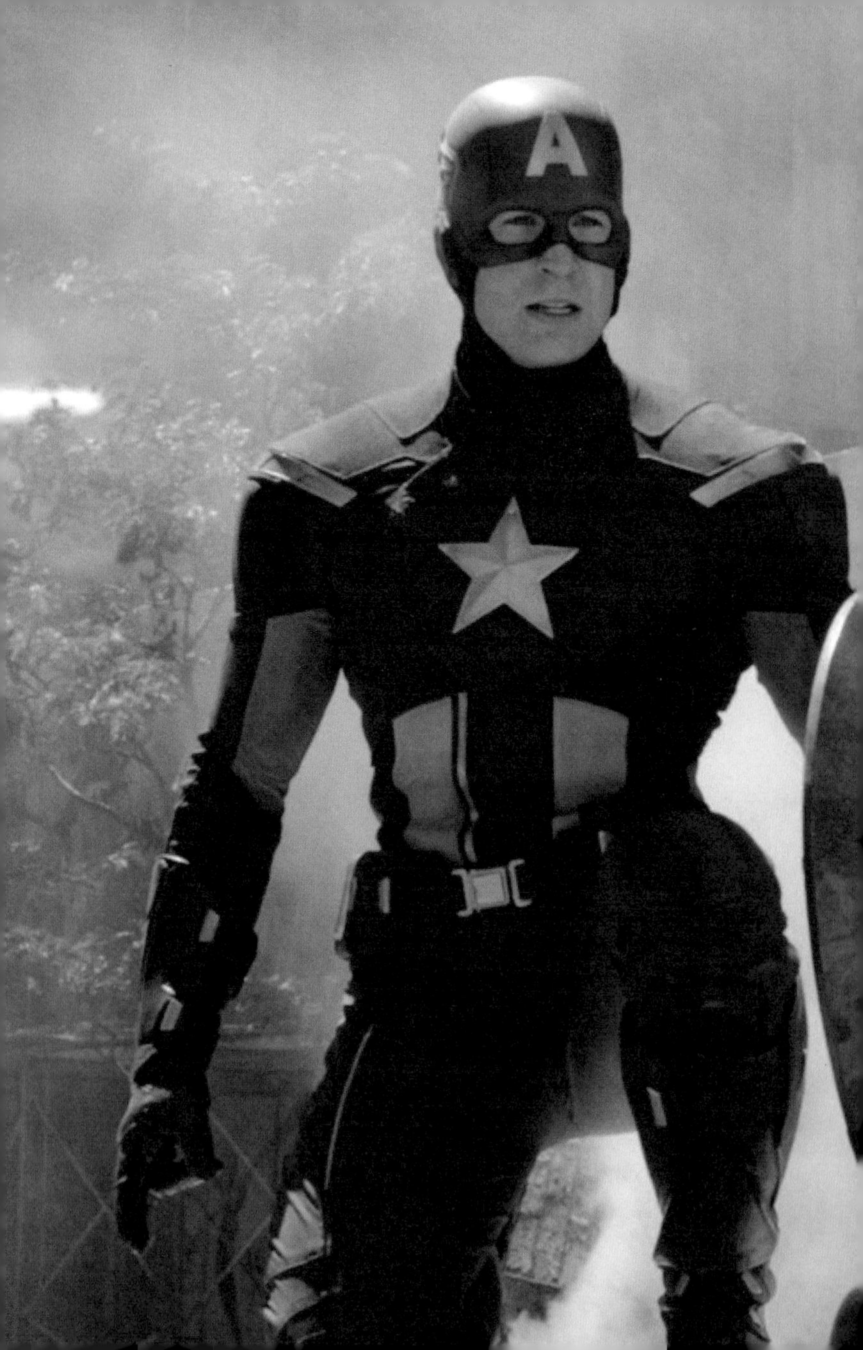

MARVEL STUDIOS

BE MORE CAPTAIN AMERICA

WRITTEN BY GLENN DAKIN

CONTENTS

TAKE THE SHIELD

Captain America is a symbol of heroism across the world. He is a fighter who doesn't know when to quit. But he is also a leader who will always try to see the best in everyone. Cap may seem on another level, but there is no reason you can't be like him. You don't have to dress up in a star-spangled costume to stand up for what you believe. Under the red, white, and blue is just a man trying to help others and be the best he can be. You can follow his example and be a hero too...

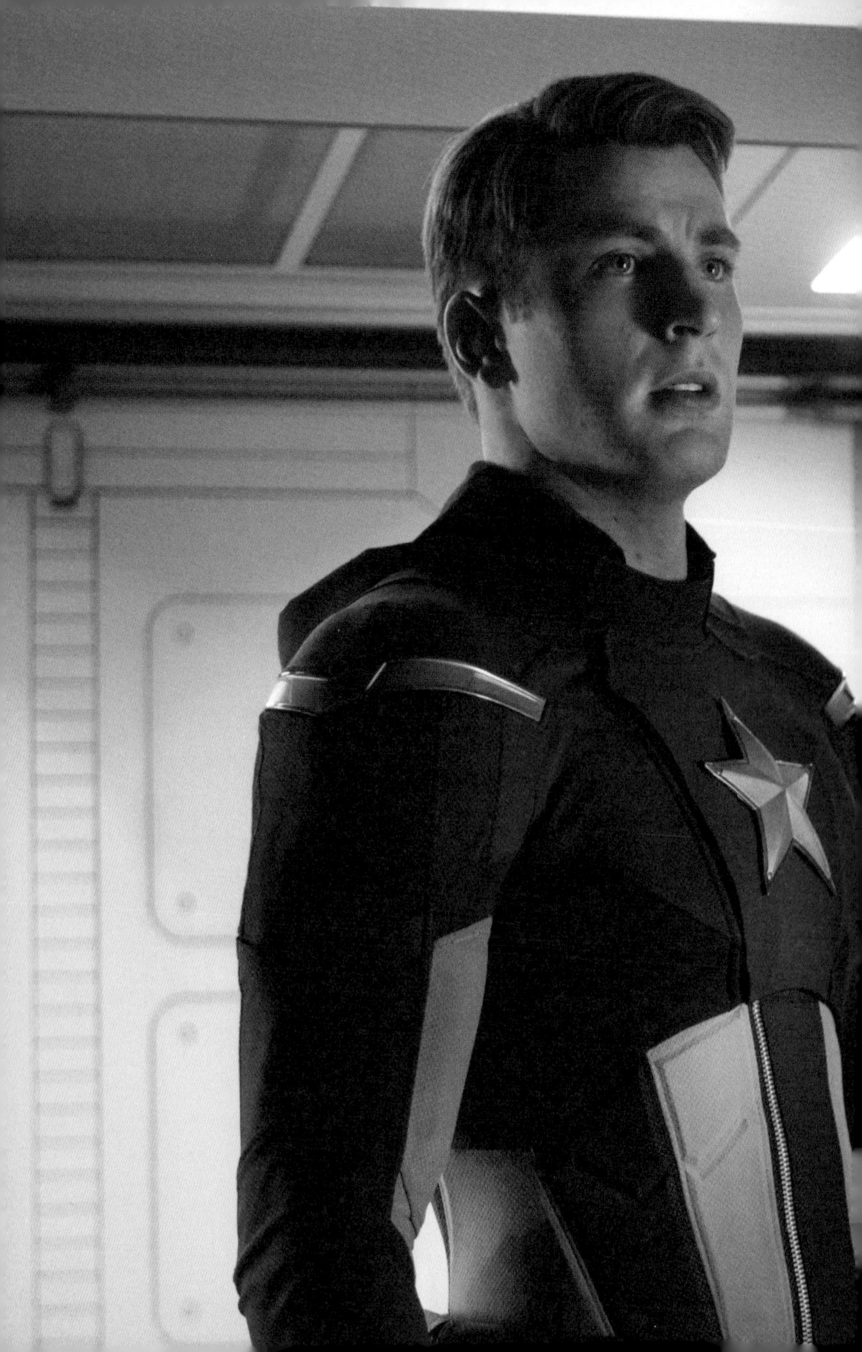

BECOME AN AVENGER

Steve Rogers was chosen to be Captain America because of who he was, deep down. He was someone who cared about doing the right thing. And that is why he became an Avenger – because an Avenger is someone who sees something wrong and puts it right. Before you get to fight any bad guys, the most important change starts with yourself.

"You start running and
they'll never let you stop."
Steve Rogers

FACE YOUR PROBLEMS

Steve Rogers may not have been the biggest guy on his block, but he never ran away from a fight – or any other kind of problem. Running away would mean losing respect for himself. Steve's strength lies in his determination and ability to work hard to succeed. Face your problems head on and they may turn out to be smaller than you thought.

"I don't like bullies.
I don't care where they're from."
Steve Rogers

KNOW YOUR ENEMY

Captain America has fought against all kinds of
enemies, from machines like Ultron to alien invaders
like Thanos. But his true enemy is one we're all
familiar with. His real foe is *the bully*. They can
exist in any area of life: school, work, the street.
The person who abuses their strength or position
to get their way – the person who needs you to feel
small so they can feel big. Most bullies are cowards,
and if you stand up to them they'll turn and run.

"Don't win the war
'till I get there!"
Steve Rogers

GET INVOLVED

In the dark days of World War II, Steve Rogers
had every reason to sit it out. He'd been rejected by
recruiting boards over and over again. But his best
pal was going to join the fight, and Steve couldn't
bear to be left out. For you, it doesn't need to be
a war. It could be a sports game, a litter-pick,
or helping out at your little sister's birthday party.
You learn more by getting involved. And you'll
build a reputation as a doer, not a talker.

"The price of freedom is high.
It always has been. And it's
a price I'm willing to pay."
Captain America

STAND UP FOR WHAT YOU BELIEVE

Nobody looks at Captain America and thinks,
"I wonder what this guy thinks about freedom of
speech". Everyone knows what Cap believes in:
peace, liberty, and the many other rights we take for
granted. They say if you stand for nothing you fall
for everything, so don't be a fall-guy. If you stand
up for what you believe, people will respect that.
They will know who you are – and won't waste
your time asking you to join Hydra.

"If you get hurt, hurt them back.
If you get killed... walk it off."
Captain America

TALK THE TALK

A big attitude goes a long way. No one wants the Avengers to come up with a bunch of dubious excuses, or for them to watch Thanos make half the universe disappear and then say, "Oh well, you win some, you lose some…" Heroes say stuff like: "let's do it", or "I'm going in!" And they mean it. Learn to make inspiring, sometimes bold remarks. Hey, your public expects it.

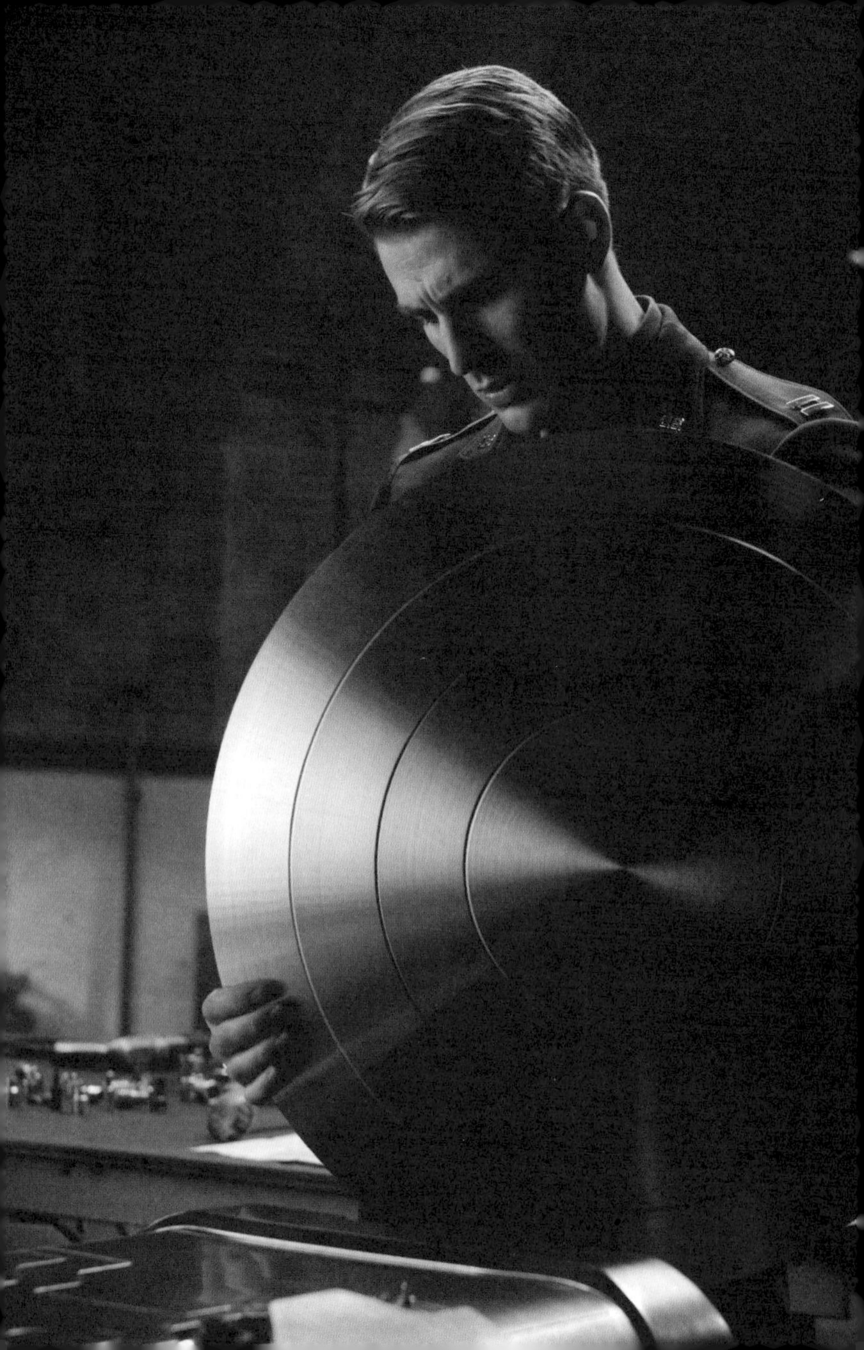

GET YOUR SHIELD

Captain America has a mighty vibranium shield he takes with him on every mission. It absorbs energy on impact and can protect him from just about anything. Now, you don't need an actual piece of metal to defend you. Your personal shield is the rules and habits you live your life by. Stick to a code and you'll have a better chance of winning life's battles.

"I'll put it on the list."
Captain America

MAKE A LIST

When Steve Rogers comes out of the ice and realises he has missed decades of cool stuff, his friends tell him to make a list of stuff to catch up on. The only problem is, everyone has a different idea of what should be on that list. Your list might not involve listening to disco music and watching the moon landing like Steve's, but having your own targets helps you to focus. So forget what your friends tell you and make your own choices. And don't rule out disco... dancing is good for you.

"Secure the engine room,
then find me a date."
Captain America

GET YOUR PRIORITIES RIGHT

While Cap and Natasha Romanoff are on a mission for S.H.I.E.L.D. to rescue a shipload of hostages, she starts to quiz him on his love life. If this has ever happened to you, you'll know it's never great when your friends try to set you up, and especially not when in a life-and-death situation. Cap has no hesitation in telling Black Widow to keep her mind on the job. Do the important stuff first – then you can enjoy the uninvited life advice later.

"If I see a situation pointed
south, I can't ignore it."
Captain America

KNOW YOURSELF

It's easy to go along with the crowd. Often the crowd is right. But what happens when you see that something is wrong, and others don't agree? Do you just look the other way? Cap doesn't. That's the way he's made, and he lets his friends know it. There is an old saying, "we can agree to disagree". Cap would rather have an honest argument than hide his opinion. And in the end – if you're like Cap – you'll be happy you fought for what you believed in.

"I can do this all day."
Captain America

NEVER GIVE UP

When you're saving the world, giving up isn't an option. You might not have to fight an angry Iron Man, or your own past-self, but you can still learn to dig deep and keep going like Cap. The trick is to be fighting for a cause you care about, like pursuing your own dream. If you are doing something you love, you really can do it all day.

"I'm home."
Captain America

KNOW WHERE YOU BELONG

Everybody needs to know where they belong.
Thor has Asgard and Black Panther has Wakanda.
But where you belong doesn't have to be a physical
place. Cap feels at home when he's with people
who want to make a difference. If people are fighting
the same fight, then they can become like family.
Home is wherever you are needed and appreciated
by those most important to you.

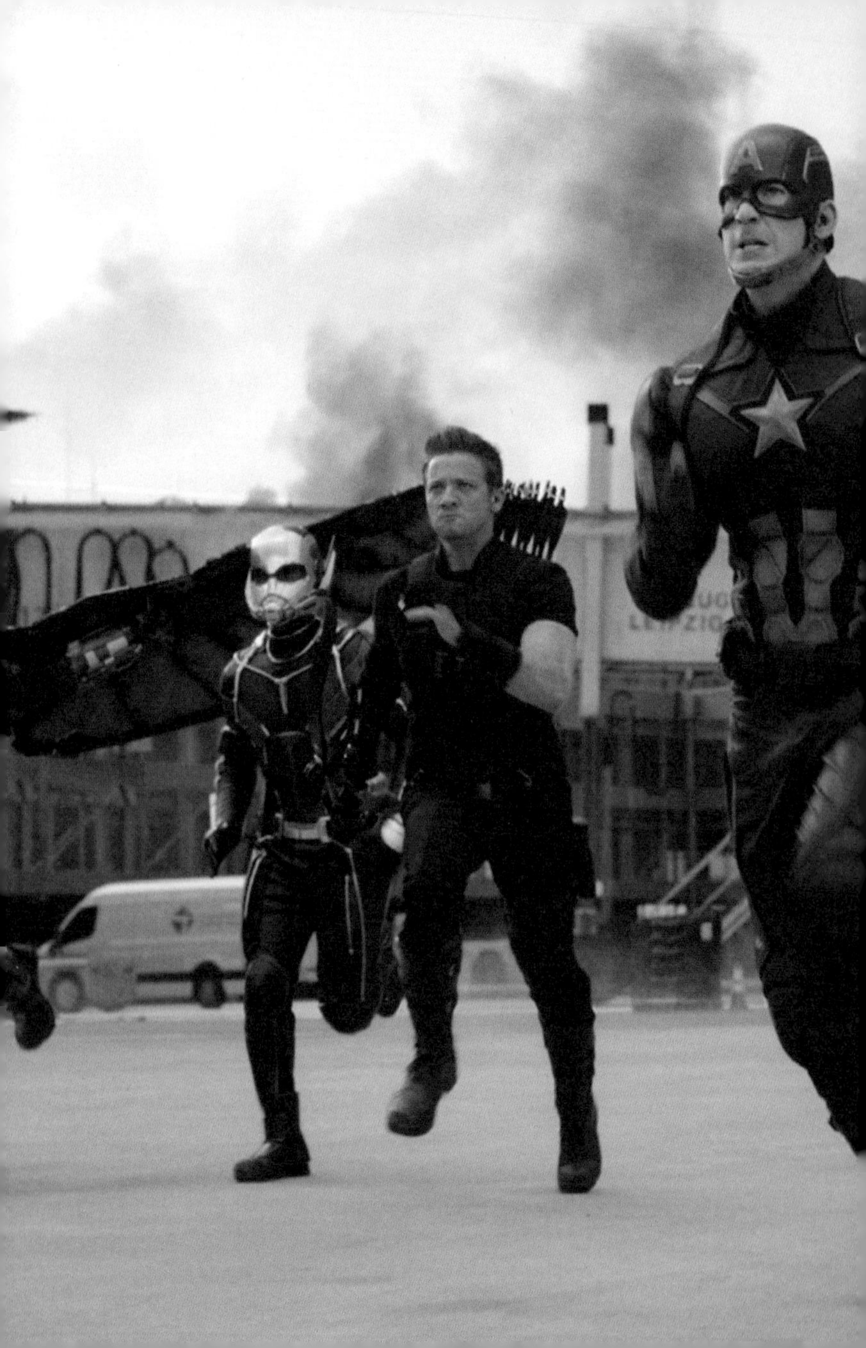

ASSEMBLE YOUR TEAM

We all need help from time to time and Cap is no exception. Someone who stands alone is easily surrounded. Turn up with friends and then at least you're not the only target! Even if you're not battling evil you'll still need allies, someone to watch your back. Your team doesn't have to contain a gamma-spawned monster or a guy that can shrink to ant-size. You might just need a friend who can make you laugh.

"Avengers Assemble!"
Captain America

MAKE THE RIGHT FRIENDS

Cap is a world-famous hero, but he doesn't surround himself with admirers and people who agree with everything he says. Cap makes friends with strong characters, people who argue with him, challenge him, and make him stronger. The right friends will tell you the truth, maybe make fun of you – like Tony Stark – but they will also stick by you to the end. Even cranky friends like the Hulk are worth keeping. Let's face it, they make even worse enemies.

"I'm with you to the
end of the line."
Captain America

BE LOYAL

Sticking by a friend when everyone else has given
up on them can mean everything to that person.
Steve Rogers stands by Bucky when the whole world
is against him. That's because Cap knows the true
Bucky, deep down. By being loyal, you will inspire
real friendship back. Show belief in your friends
when they mess up – because tomorrow the one
in need of help might be you.

"This isn't freedom. This is fear."
Captain America

SPEAK UP
FOR YOURSELF

We are all told to tell the truth, but sometimes it's the hardest thing to say. Especially to a friend. When S.H.I.E.L.D. creates a squadron of helicarriers with missiles aimed at all the enemies of freedom in the world, Cap is not impressed. He only sees a world ruled by fear of violence, and isn't afraid to say so. But that's what makes him a hero. Don't hold back when something needs to be said. Sometimes one honest word can be the start of change.

"Wait, are you talking about
a time machine?"
Captain America

USE THE SKILLS OF THOSE AROUND YOU

When you've assembled your team, use its players wisely. Play to their strengths. You may want to tackle Loki, but maybe Thor knows him better. You might want to hit that distant target, but maybe Hawkeye is the right call for that job. Ant-Man's ideas might sound far-fetched, but they could mean the difference between defeat and victory. Your team will be happier if you let people do what they're good at.

"This doesn't have to end
in a fight, Buck."
Captain America

KNOW THAT FIGHTING ISN'T ALWAYS THE ANSWER

You've trained and prepared and psyched yourself up
for a fight. Now, guess what? Don't have it. The aim
of being a hero is to make a better world for others.
That can't be achieved if the world becomes a
battleground. If a fight – any fight – can be avoided,
it's the wiser option. Cap has all the experience to
beat the Winter Soldier in battle, but then he might
lose a friend. Sometimes the worst thing you
can do in a fight, is win it.

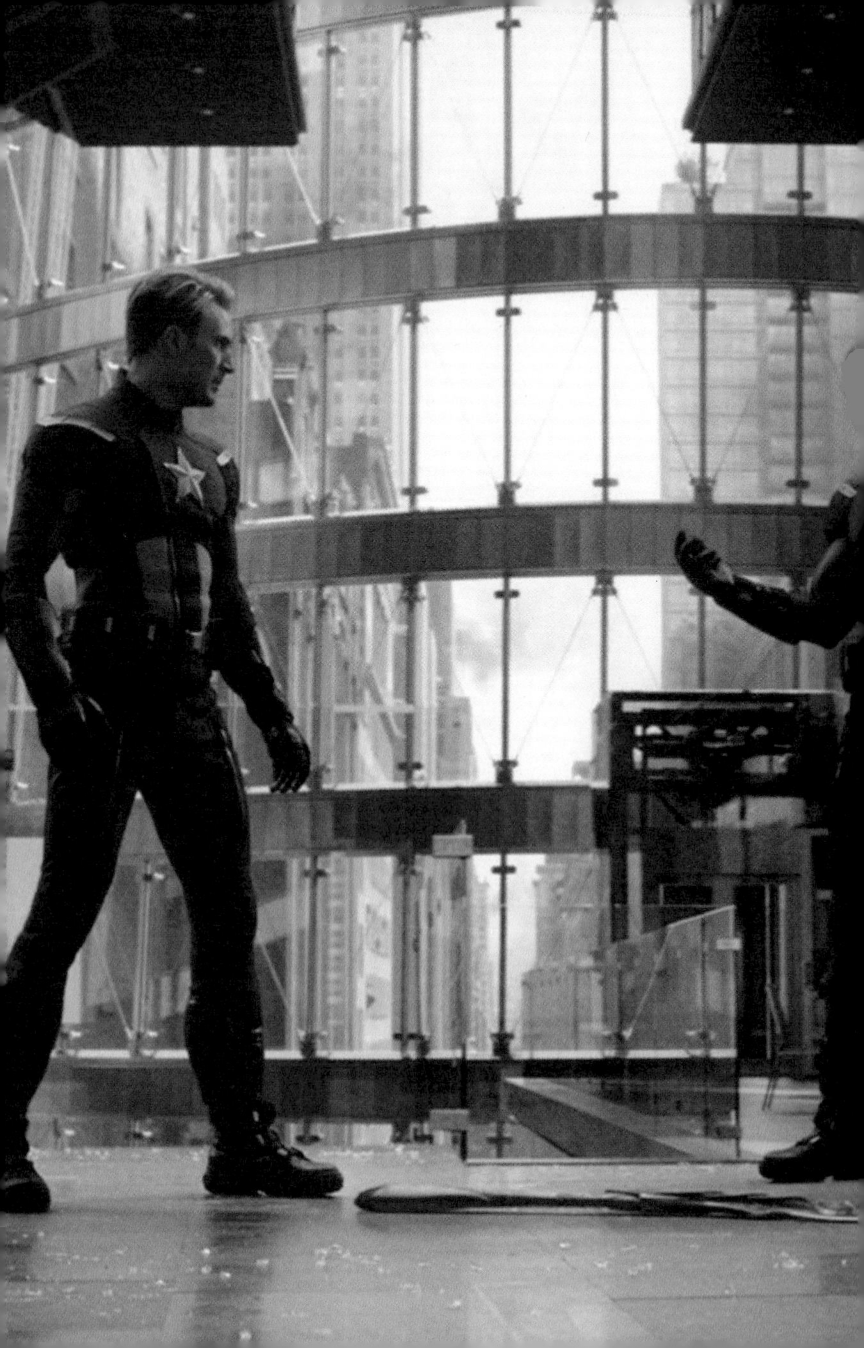

STAY TRUE TO YOURSELF

People think a hero is someone who is perfect, invincible, and who always does the right thing. Captain America would say he is none of these things – deep down he's just an ordinary guy. Cap can get by without perfection, because he's happy with his true self. He's old-fashioned, but courteous and humble. He brings these values wherever he goes. That way he always feels at home.

"I got beat up in that alley.
And that parking lot.
And behind that diner."
Steve Rogers

ADMIT YOUR FAILINGS

Steve Rogers never tries to hide the fact that he was once the neighbourhood punchbag. In fact, he grew up a skinny kid who others could knock down. The point is, he always got straight back up. Being honest about your failures is a strength. It reminds you to do better, keeps you motivated, and shows others that you are only human. Remember, losing a few fights along the way doesn't stop you from winning the battle.

"I'd offer to cook you dinner, but you seem pretty miserable already."
Captain America

JUST BE YOU

It's OK to have bad days, but staying true to who you are will help you and your friends get through them. Even in the dark times after Thanos makes half the world disappear, Steve Rogers keeps the remaining Avengers in good spirits by making fun of his own flaws. When it gets tough, remember to just be yourself. Your friends will appreciate it (even if they don't appreciate your cooking).

"Put on the suit!"
Captain America

FIGHT FAIR

When Captain America gets angry at Iron Man
(under the influence of Loki's sceptre) he won't start
a fight with Tony until Tony suits up. Well, Cap has his
power all the time, but Tony has to put his armour on.
It's part of Cap's code. Fair play cuts both ways. If you
expect people to be fair to you, you have to treat them
the same way. Sometimes you might have to throw
away a great advantage to keep your reputation.

"I'm just a kid from Brooklyn."
Captain America

REMEMBER WHERE YOU'VE COME FROM

No matter how far you've come, it's important to stop and take a look back at where you started. Cap wasn't born a Super Soldier – he had a childhood filled with illness and loss. But that gave him humility and made him appreciate the things he did have – an outlook he kept after he became Captain America. If you take the time to remember where you've come from, you'll appreciate where you are all the more.

"I thought maybe I'll try some of that life that Tony was telling me to get."
Steve Rogers

FOLLOW YOUR HEART

After the battle with Thanos, when Cap has returned
the Infinity Stones to their right place in time, he takes
advantage of time travel to return to his original era.
There, he reunites with Peggy Carter, the woman he
loves. Well, Tony did tell him to get a life, and you have
to listen to Iron Man! In your quest to be more Captain
America, never forget to also be a human being, and
not let anything stand in the way of your dreams.

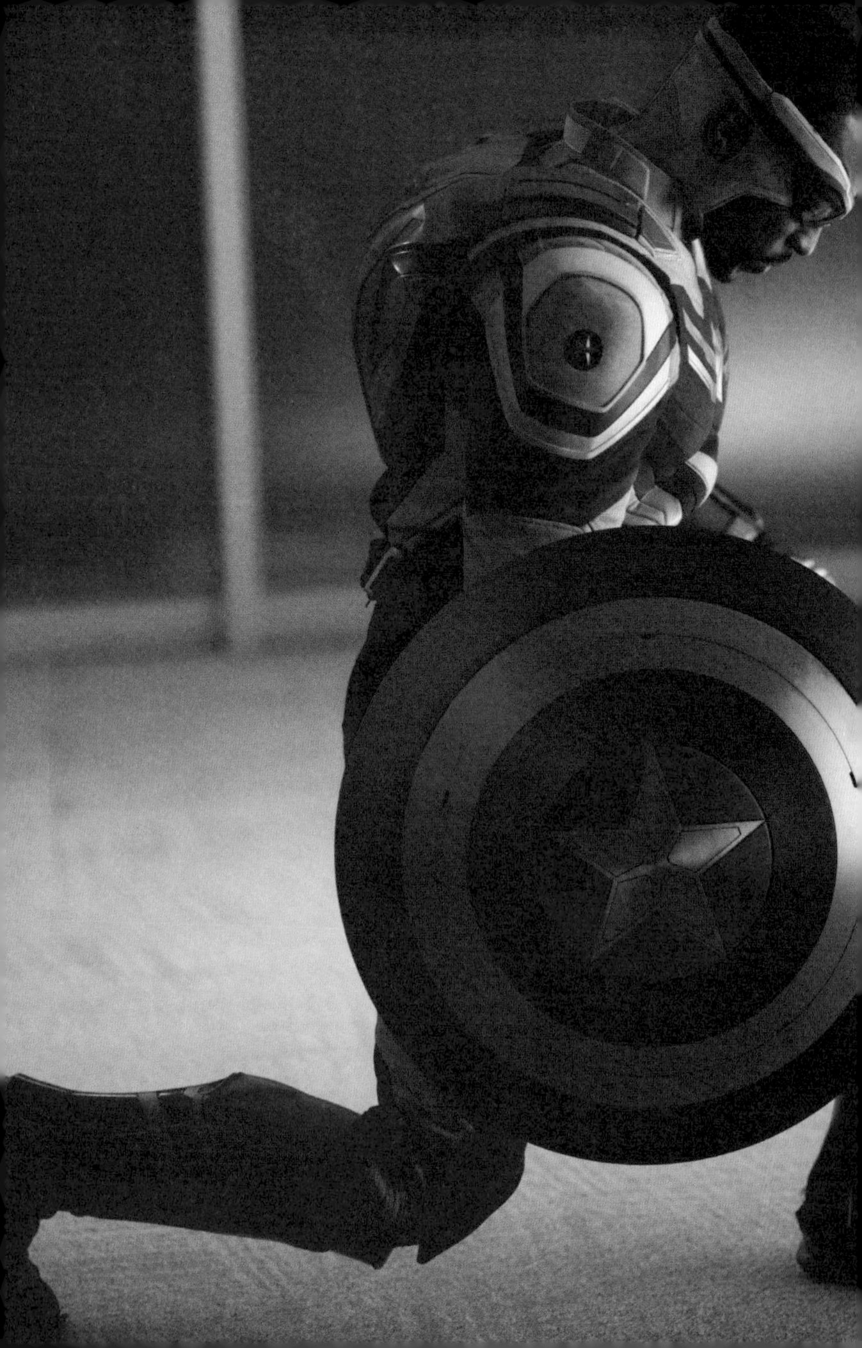

TAKE UP THE CHALLENGE

New times need new heroes. Steve Rogers helped keep Thanos, Ultron, and Loki at bay. Now he has passed the name – and the shield – along. Sam Wilson didn't celebrate when he was given the chance. He took time to weigh the responsibility. That's because Captain America isn't just a name or a costume – it's a legacy. Sam needed to understand that legacy before taking the job. Like Sam, you can achieve big things if you believe in yourself.

"You've gotta step up."
Captain America

BE READY

It's nice to wait for the perfect time, isn't it? We all like to have that little extra preparation before we handle the big test, important race, or asking someone out on a date... the trouble is, sometimes, the time doesn't wait for you. It just arrives, and there it is, putting you on the spot. This is when you might not feel ready. But if you stop and think, your whole life has led you to this moment – trust your instincts and you may find that you are ready after all.

"You gotta stop looking to other people to tell you who you are."
Captain America

DECIDE WHO YOU WANT TO BE

Do you have an idea in your head of who you are?
If so, who put that idea there... you, or someone else?
We all grow up with ideas of what we can do and who
we can be. Don't let other people decide those things
for you. Sam didn't feel ready to be Captain America
at first, but then he met the challenge. *He* decided
who he wanted to be – not the government, not the
neighbourhood, not even the Winter Soldier.

"Do the work."
Captain America

WORK HARD

There's no magical, easy way to be a hero. If you're looking for easy, perhaps being more Captain America isn't for you. And sometimes in life it can be a struggle just being an ordinary person. There's something heroic in that too. Whether you're fighting the Flag Smashers on live TV, helping the family business, or just earning someone's trust, there's always one thing you have to do: the hard work.

"I'm trying something different."
Captain America

DO IT YOUR WAY

Have you ever tried to copy your heroes? It doesn't quite work out, does it? Maybe the originals succeeded because they didn't copy anyone. They were themselves. If you want to stand out, it's time to do things your way. When the Falcon becomes Captain America he brings his own eye-catching style. And he sees no reason to clip his wings, either. Sam makes sure that the bad guys have some new tricks to cope with.

"The only power I have is that
I believe we can do better."
Captain America

BELIEVE IN A BETTER WAY

When Sam becomes Captain America, he has no superpowers, no serum that gives him the edge over others. He only has what he has always had, a determination to be the best he can be. He didn't get his strength in any lab, or from a radioactive accident. It all comes from his beliefs. And that means you can find that strength, too. To truly be more Captain America... believe in a better way.

Senior Editor David Fentiman
Project Art Editor Stefan Georgiou
Senior Production Editor Jennifer Murray
Senior Production Controller Mary Slater
Managing Editor Sarah Harland
Managing Art Editor Vicky Short
Publishing Director Mark Searle

DK would like to thank: Sarah Beers, Adam Davis, Erika Denton, Sofia Finamore,
Vincent Garcia, Keilah Jordan, Tiffany Mau, Julio Palacol, Ariel Shasteen, and
Jennifer Wojnar at Marvel Studios; Chelsea Alon at Disney Publishing;
and Lauren Nesworthy for proofreading.

AVAILABLE NOW ON VARIOUS FORMATS INCLUDING DIGITAL WHERE APPLICABLE FOR THE
FOLLOWING FILMS AND DISNEY+ ORIGINAL SERIES: Captain America: The First Avenger,
Marvel's The Avengers, Captain America: The Winter Soldier, Avengers: Age of Ultron,
Captain America: Civil War, Avengers: Endgame, The Falcon and the Winter Soldier
© 2021 MARVEL

First published in Great Britain in 2021 by
Dorling Kindersley Limited
DK, One Embassy Gardens, 8 Viaduct Gardens,
London SW11 7BW
A Penguin Random House Company

The authorised representative in the EEA is
Dorling Kindersley Verlag GmbH. Arnulfstr. 124,
80636 Munich, Germany

© 2021 MARVEL

10 9 8 7 6 5 4 3 2 1
001–325113–Nov/2021

A CIP catalogue record for this book
is available from the British Library.

ISBN: 978-0-24151-627-0

Printed and bound in China

For the curious
www.dk.com

MIX
Paper from
responsible sources
FSC™ C018179

This book was made with Forest
Stewardship Council ™ certified
paper - one small step in DK's
commitment to a sustainable
future. For more information go to
www.dk.com/our-green-pledge

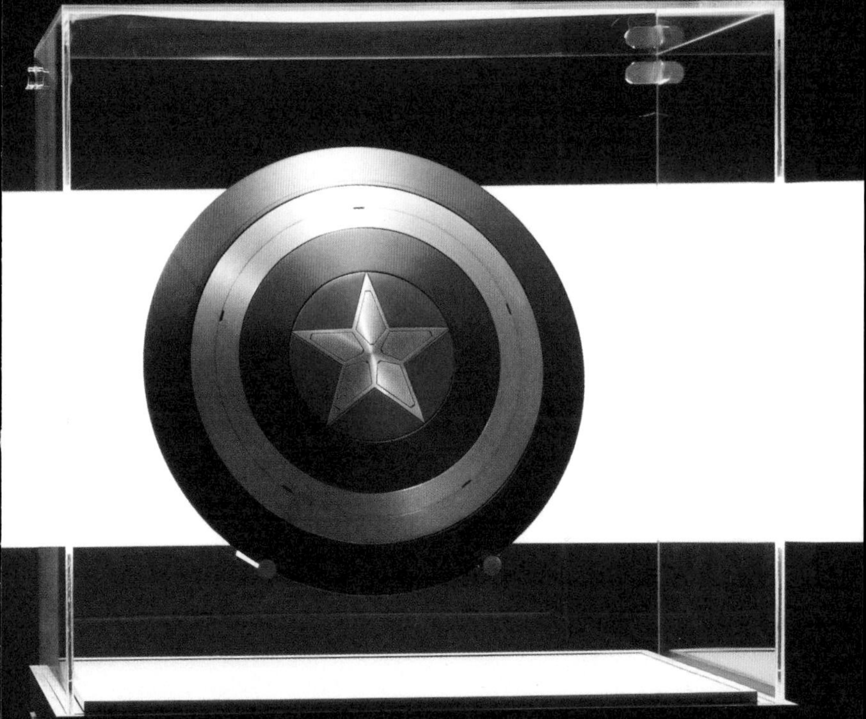